Theme Parks

Christine Butterworth

Series Editors: Steve Barlow and Steve Skidmore

Published by Ginn and Company
Halley Court Jordan Hill Oxford OX2 8EJ
A division of Reed Educational and Professional Publishing Ltd

Telephone number for ordering **Impact**: 01865 888084

OXFORD MELBOURNE AUCKLAND JOHANNESBURG BLANTYRE
GABORONE IBADAN PORTSMOUTH (NH) USA CHICAGO

First published 1999

2003 2002 2001 2000 99

10 9 8 7 6 5 4 3 2 1

ISBN 0 435 21230 3

Illustrations
Keith Page, Temple Rogers

Picture research
Thelma Gilbert

Cover photographs
Foreground: Images Colour Library. Background: Image Bank

Designed by Shireen Nathoo Design

Printed and bound in Spain by Eldelvives

Acknowledgements
Special thanks to Andy Nichols of Nichols, Brown and Webber; to John Wardley, and to the 1997/8 students who helped me at Homerswood School, Welwyn Garden City; also to all the people who contributed to the preparation of material in this book.

Every effort has been made to contact owners of copyright material, but if any have been inadvertently overlooked, the publisher will be pleased to make the necessary arrangements at the first opportunity.

The Authors and Publishers wish to thank the following for permission to reproduce photographs on the pages noted:
Ace Photo Library pp.7, 16; Alton Towers p.43; AP p.25; Barry Norman/WKVL pp.8,32; Cedar Point/D Feicht p.40; Chessington World of Adventures pp.4, 13, 26, 28, 29, 30; Collections/Neil Calladine p.17 (*bottom*); Collections/Sam Walsh p.37; Colorific/Catherine Karnow p.5; Colorific/Lee Battaglia p.17 (*centre*); Corbis p.33; Corbis/Bettmann p.35; European Coaster Club pp.19, 20, 41; Image Bank pp.10-11, 16 (*top*), 17 (*top*), 44; Katz/I Dean Life Mag@Time Inc p.9; Katz/Randy G Taylor/ICS p.45; Nottingham Central Library pp.6-7; Popperfoto p.24; Popperfoto/Reuters p.23; Port Aventura p.14 (*bottom*); Rex Features pp.4, 12, 21, 36; Rex Features/Peter Brook p.14 (*top right*); Rex Features/Universal Studios p.14 (*top left*); Stratosphere Tower Hotel p.39.

Tel: 01865 888058 email: info.he@heinemann.co.uk

Contents

Introduction

A theme park is more than just a funfair. It has lots of rides. But it also makes visitors feel part of a 'theme' or story.

Each year, 20 million people in Britain go to theme parks. They spend 250 million pounds.

Top theme parks in Britain

1 Alton Towers. Nearly three million people go there every year.
2 Chessington World of Adventures. Nearly two million people go there every year.
3 Legoland. Around one and a half million people go there every year.

▼ Chessington World of Adventures.

▲ Alton Towers.

Every year, three million people travel from Britain to visit theme parks.

Top theme parks for visitors from Britain

1   Walt Disney World in Florida, America.
2   Disneyland Paris, France.
3   Universal Studios in California, America.
4   Port Aventura near Barcelona, Spain.

▼ *Universal Studios, California.*

Why do theme parks attract so many visitors? Find out how theme parks work and why people enjoy them so much.

The first theme parks and fairs

FUN!

People go to theme parks and fairs to have fun.

The first fairs were big markets. People went to buy and sell. They also went to meet their friends and have a good time.

Nottingham had its first Goose Fair almost 800 years ago. Farmers put 'shoes' of tar and sand on the feet of their geese. Then the geese walked to market in Nottingham.

▼ *Nottingham Goose Fair in Victorian times.*

▲ *Nottingham Goose Fair today. It is now a huge funfair.*

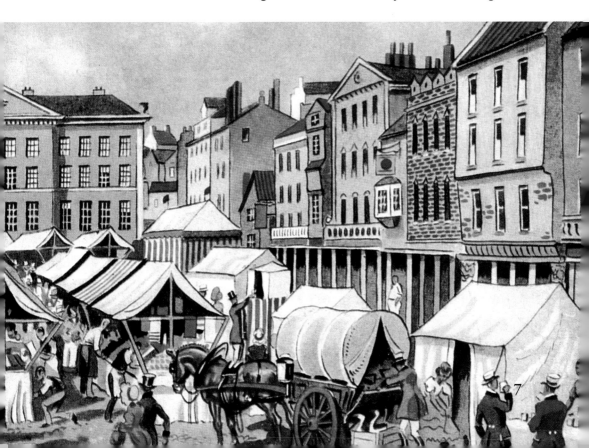

FASTER!

Electricity was first discovered in 1829. Funfairs began to use electricity to make faster rides in the 1870s.

The first big wheel was built in Chicago in 1893. It was 76 metres high. People loved the fast rides. By 1895, more people went to fairs than ever before.

▲ *The first big wheel in 1893.*

TV AND FILM STARS

Funfairs spread through America and Europe. But, in 1953, television became popular. Many people stopped going to fairs and watched TV instead. It looked as if funfairs would die out.

Then, in 1955, Walt Disney opened Disneyland in California. It had fast rides. But it also copied the scenes and stars that people watched on TV. People started going to fairs again. The modern theme park was born.

▲ *Disneyland, California.*

How is a theme park made?

PLANNING A THEME PARK

A theme park is carefully planned. The designer of the theme
park needs to find out:

- How many people live near the theme park.
- How many people live a short drive away.
- The age of those people.
- What sort of rides they will want.

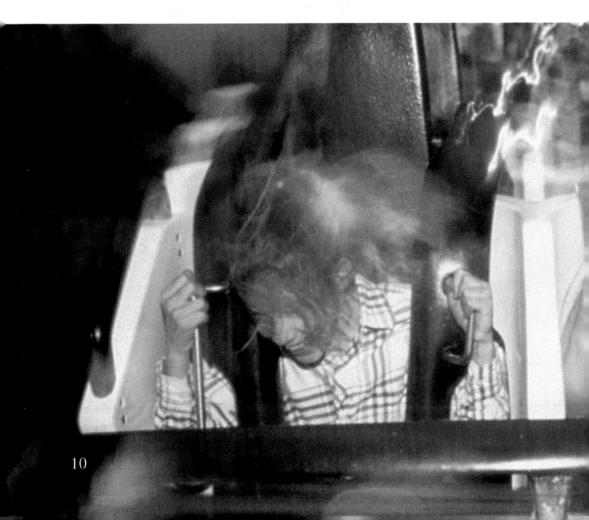

10

The park has to be big enough for the number of people who may come. Nearly 1,000 people can 'fit' into a space the size of a football pitch.

The rides must attract people who live nearby. Young children need slower rides. Families like water rides. Teenagers enjoy scary 'white-knuckle' rides.

▼ *A white-knuckle ride at Grand Slam Canyon, USA.*

DESIGNING A THEME PARK

There are two basic designs for a theme park.

1 Wheel-shape design

Visitors start at the centre of the wheel. Then they walk out to the different areas around the wheel.

▼ *Disneyland Paris has a wheel-shape design.*

2 Pathway design

Visitors follow a path. Big rides are put at the edge of the park.
People visit the smaller rides on their way to the bigger rides.

▼ *Chessington World of Adventures has a pathway design.*

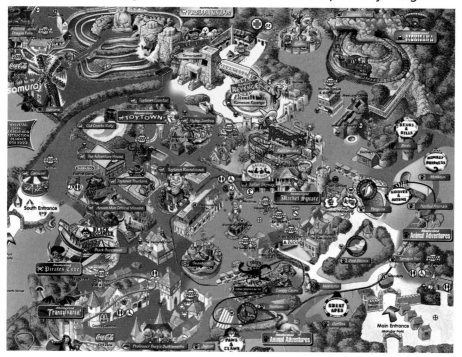

DID YOU KNOW?

In one year, visitors at Chessington drank 1,995,462
regular Cokes. They ate:
- 200 tonnes of chips
- 7 tonnes of fish
- 22 tonnes of burgers.

STAGE 3 CHOOSING THEMES

The designer asks local people what themes they want to see in the park. People often ask for:

- aliens from outer space
- characters and places from films and TV
- scenes of faraway lands.

▼ *Back to the future ride.*

▼ *Polynesian ride at Port Aventura.*

▲ *Jurassic Park ride.*

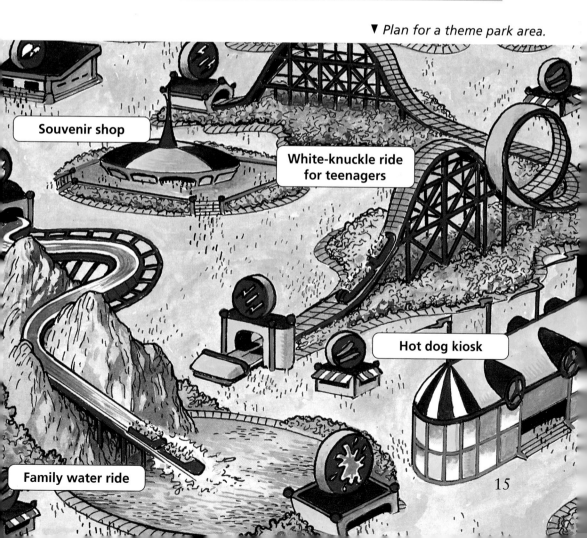

STAGE 4 PUTTING IT TOGETHER

The designer needs to plan each themed area in the park.

DID YOU KNOW?

Each themed area must have:
- at least two rides
- somewhere to buy food
- shops selling gifts.

▼ *Plan for a theme park area.*

Souvenir shop

White-knuckle ride for teenagers

Hot dog kiosk

Family water ride

15

Taken for a ride!

KINDS OF RIDE

There are five main kinds of ride at a theme park: roller coasters, round rides, swing rides, water rides and dark rides.

▲ *Roller coasters.*

► *Round rides.*

16

▲ Swing rides.

◄ Water rides.

► Dark rides.

MAKING A RIDE

It takes two kinds of expert to think up a ride, the ride designer and the engineer.

The ride designer:

- Thinks what kind of ride people want.
- Works out how much the ride will cost.
- Works out the safety details.
- Plans the scenery, lights and music.

The engineer:

- Helps the designer know what *can* be built.
- Builds the machinery.

The final design is shown to the local council. They have to give the go-ahead to build the ride.

DID YOU KNOW?

Some rides in theme parks are ready-made. But the most famous rides are made specially. They cost millions of pounds to build and are top secret until they open.

MEET A TOP RIDE DESIGNER

John Wardley designs rides for Britain's biggest theme parks. He designed *Oblivion* and *Nemesis* for Alton Towers. He talked to us about his work.

Q: What's the secret of a good ride?

A: A good ride scares you stiff, but it doesn't last long. It has to be fun! It's like the thrill of bungee-jumping, but you're strapped safely into the ride.

Q: What was new about the idea for *Oblivion* at Alton Towers?

A: *Oblivion* is the first roller coaster in the world that just drops straight down. You can't see down the hole before you drop into it. The ride cost 13 million pounds to build.

▼ Oblivion *at Alton Towers.*

Q: Out of all the rides you've designed, which is your favourite?

A: *Nemesis*, the overhead roller coaster at Alton Towers. Designing and building it was a very happy time.

▲ Nemesis *at Alton Towers.*

Q: What's your ambition?

A: I want to go on making amazing rides. It's great to know that millions of people enjoy my rides each year.

Safety facts

CROWD CONTROL!

Theme parks are designed to be safe when full of people.
Visitors follow paths around the rides so that crowds
don't build up in one place. Exit paths can be opened if
people need to get out quickly. Staff are trained to manage
the crowds.

TESTING THE RIDES

The rides are faster but safer than ever. Every ride has its
own set of safety rules. All rides have their brakes tested
every day. Different kinds of safety checks are made weekly,
monthly and yearly. Each ride is taken to bits every year.
Its parts are tested and new parts are put in.

DID YOU KNOW?

Staff are also trained to help with medical emergencies.
At Alton Towers, the staff helped a woman who was giving
birth. The parents gave the baby the name Alton!

A theme park can be seven times safer than a car ride. Most accidents happen because people make mistakes, not because machines go wrong. Safety in British theme parks is very good.

PAST DISASTERS

Accidents happened in the past because safety checks were not as strict as they are now.

▼ *London, May 1972.*

DEATH TRAP BIG COASTER

The worst British funfair disaster ever

The brakes failed on the roller coaster at a Battersea funfair yesterday. Five children were killed.

"The cars just slid back and rolled down the steep slope. The children were thrown out," said the father of one of the children who was killed.

A survivor of the accident said, "I saw the man holding the brake. His face was white and I knew something was wrong.

"The car came off the rails and that was the last thing I knew. I am lucky to be alive."

RIDERS HANG IN MID-AIR

Safety straps stop them plunging to ground

A loop-the-loop ride in a Brussels funfair got stuck yesterday. The ride jammed at the top of the first loop.

Twenty-six people hung upside down for one and a half hours.

Firefighters had to go up ladders to rescue them. No one was hurt, but they were all very shocked.

▲ *Belgium, August 1997.*

Working in a theme park

Three of the staff at Chessington World of Adventures describe a day at work.

MARK BANT ENTERTAINER **Age: 24**

I learned to juggle when I joined a circus at the age of 15. My job at Chessington is very busy, but I love meeting people. You can't make people happy if you don't enjoy your job.

9.00am   I go to work, shower and get into costume.Then I go down to the entry gates and greet people. I juggle for them.

11.00am   I eat breakfast – at last! Then I ride my unicycle round the park. My job is to make sure people don't get too bored waiting for a ride.

12.00pm   I do my show in the centre of the park. I pretend I'm a crazy chef – I set my frying pan on fire. My job is to help people have a good time. If a ride breaks down, then I help keep people happy.

1.00pm   I eat lunch. Then I go and entertain some more queues on the busy rides. I juggle and do some fire-eating.

5.00pm   Time to go home, but my day's not over yet. I've got an evening show in another park tonight!

HARRY SPILLET TECHNICAL SUPERVISOR **Age: 21**

This is my first job, and Chessington is a brilliant place to work. I like solving technical problems. I'd like to go on to become a technical supervisor at rock concerts.

 9.30am I power up the sound system. I look after all the lighting and sound equipment in the park. The equipment here is worth about a million pounds. I also check that the times of that day's shows are up on the board.

10.30am I go and switch on the sound system for the animal shows. I also do repairs and odd jobs.

 1.00pm Lunchtime.

 2.00pm It's time for the open-air show. I look after the microphone and play the music.

 3.00pm I go to the circus show early, to give the acts their calls. I control the sound and lighting for the show. I also work the trap-door that brings the dancers up from under the stage.

▼ *A technical supervisor at work in Sealion Bay, Chessington.*

LOUISE RAWLINSON RIDE OPERATOR **Age: 20**

I've been a ride operator for two years, and I love it. How many jobs do you get where you can spin people around? At school I wasn't good at reading, but I love working with people here.

9.00am My team and I clean the ride before we open it.

 10.00am I go to the control box to open the ride. I have buttons that start and stop it. If there's a fault, I hit a big red Emergency button to cut off the power.

 11.30am I'll have a break. I'm trained to operate all the rides now.

The most difficult ride to operate is a big coaster, like the *Vampire*. I watch the cars on a row of TV screens. I flick between the screens, keeping an eye on the track. This job is very stressful, and if I get the timing wrong the ride will stop itself.

 5.00pm Going-home time in the winter. In the summer I work until 9.00pm!

▼ The Vampire, *Chessington.*

Roller coasters

THE FIRST ROLLER COASTERS

Many people love roller coaster rides most of all. Some roller coasters even have their own fan clubs! But coasters are not such a new idea.

Two hundred and fifty years ago, people built ice slides in Russia. Sledges swooped up and down ice slopes 20 metres high.

▼ *An ice slide in Russia.*

In the 1840s, the first loop-the-loop railway was built in Paris. People who rode it were rolled upside-down in a nine-metre circle.

▼ *The loop-the-loop railway in Paris.*

UPS AND DOWNS!

Early coasters were not very fast. Then a wheel was made that fixed the cars to the track. The coasters got faster and the drops got steeper.

The early years of the twentieth century were a great time for coasters. Every park wanted a bigger and faster one. The most famous roller coaster was the *Cyclone*. It was built in 1927, at Coney Island in America. People stood in a queue for four hours to ride the *Cyclone*.

By 1934 the *Tornado* coaster at Coney Island was also popular.

DID YOU KNOW?

Rage on the coasters. The wait for a ride on the *Cyclone* was long and hot. More than one person who tried to push in the queue was murdered!

Love on the coasters. The coasters were fast and fun. Some people loved coasters so much that they even got married on them!

The Tornado *at Coney Island in* ►
April 1934. Over 300,000 people
went to Coney Island in one day.

THE LATEST COASTERS

Designers made coasters do new things in the 1970s. They used discoveries made by scientists who worked on jet planes. A race began to make the scariest but safest rides.

Disney World in America had an indoor coaster that was a dark ride in space. The *Shuttle Loop* was made in Germany. This was a train that went from 0–95kph in three seconds and turned upside-down.

Coasters were also built that could loop-the-loop and turn around in a spiral at the same time.

▲ *One of the latest coasters looping-the-loop.*

The most famous old coaster is the *Cyclone* at Coney Island, New York. It was built in 1927 and is 25 metres high.

One of the world's highest coasters is the *High Roller*, Las Vegas, America. It was built 300 metres up on top of the Stratosphere Tower.

One of the great new UK coasters is *The Big One* at Blackpool Pleasure Beach. It is 70 metres high and goes at a speed of 130kph.

▲ The Big One, *Blackpool Pleasure Beach.*

Roller coasters on the Web!

COASTER FACTS

Coaster fans can find the latest news about coasters on computers.

The **World Wide Web** has pages that are all about coasters. The next few pages show you the sorts of things you can find at the address below.

One Web site address is:

http://dir.yahoo.com/Entertainment/Amusement_and_Theme_Parks/Roller_Coasters

▼ *The coasters page shows you what information is on the site.*

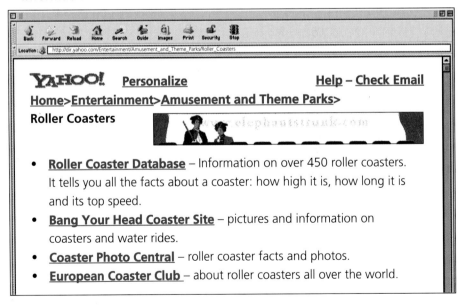

Fans can click on the Roller Coaster Database to get more facts about over 450 roller coasters.

▼ *From the Database page on the* High Roller *coaster, USA.*

High Roller: Enjoy the View

The High Roller runs round the top of the Stratosphere Tower, Las Vegas.

Admission
Tower admission: $6
Individual ride rate: $6

Hours
Weekdays: 10 am to midnight
Weekends: 10 am to 1 am

Length: 300 metres
Height: 280 metres
Biggest drop: 9 metres
Maximum speed: 50kph

Rating: 2

COASTER FANS

Coaster fans can find great pictures on the Web. There are also video clips of some coaster rides.

▼ *Photo of the week. More photos can be found*
by clicking on Coaster Photo Central.

Coaster fans can also join a fan club.

The American Coaster Club is the biggest. It has 5,000 members. The European Coaster Club has its own page on the Web.

▼ *What's on offer at the European Coaster Club site.*

Location: http://ds.dial.pipex.com/ecc/

Official Web Site

Roller coaster news, pictures and features

For members of the <u>European Coaster Club</u> (ECC) and all other fans of roller coasters and white-knuckle rides the world over.

EEC Club Pages:
- How to join the Club
- The Club magazine: The First Drop
- First Drop online
- Park trips for Club members
- Special offers for Club members

Pictures and Videos
Roller Coaster News

You are heading for Oblivion, Alton Towers, UK

Theme parks and the future

A DIFFERENT WORLD!

Theme parks will get even bigger in the future. People will visit theme parks more often. More people will go abroad to visit theme parks in other countries.

More people will spend whole holidays at parks. They will stay at special hotels in rooms that are part of the theme.

Theme parks will put on bigger and better shows in the evening.

DID YOU KNOW?

Disney have opened some themed hotels near their theme parks. You can eat, drink and sleep sport in Disney's *The All Star Sports Resort Hotel*. It has five themed buildings:

- football
- baseball
- basketball
- tennis
- surfing.

▲ *A themed hotel at Alton Towers.*

RIDES IN TIME AND SPACE

Some rides in future will take groups of people anywhere in time and space.

Computers will control the rides. They will be **virtual reality rides** where people feel part of the action shown on a computer screen.

Sounds and smells will make the action seem even more real.

A virtual reality ride. ▶

DID YOU KNOW?

Soon, no one will have to stand in a queue at a theme park. When people arrive, they will tell a computer which rides they want to go on. They will have a list of their rides on a ticket. People will then be told when it is their turn. This is called a **virtual queue**.

BIGGER AND BETTER!

Rides will be faster and higher in future. They will be made from new materials that will not wear out. Ride designers will use even bigger wheels. Rides will reach new top speeds!

New theme parks are being built all over the world. The theme parks of the future will be bigger and better than ever before.

Glossary

browser A computer program that means you can read information on the Web. *page 40*

download To copy information from the Web into your computer. *page 40*

pathway design Visitors follow a path around a theme park. Big rides are put at the edge of the park. People visit smaller rides on the way to bigger rides. *page 13*

QuickTime plug-in A computer program which means you can see moving pictures on your computer. *page 40*

virtual queue People's names go on a list in a computer. The computer tells each person when their turn comes. This means people do not have to wait in a line. They can do other things as they wait. *page 44*

virtual reality ride Riders stay in one place and wear a headset. The headset gives them the sounds, pictures and motion of a real ride. It is like being on a real ride but can take people through time and space. *page 44*

wheel-shape design Visitors walk around the theme park starting from the centre of the wheel. They visit different areas around the wheel. *page 12*

World Wide Web Also called the Web or the Internet. Many computers are joined together by telephone links. It means people have fast access to a lot of information. *page 38*

Index